Surviving Loss

2018 ©Busisiwe Mahlangu
All rights reserved
Published in Tshwane, South Africa,
by impepho press in 2018
impephopress.co.za
ISBN 978-0-6399465-3-5

Edited by Vangile Gantsho
Cover and layout by Tanya Pretorius
Proofread by Sarah Godsell and Mjele Msimang

Print Production by [•] squareDot Media
Printing by LawPrint

Earlier versions of some poems in this book have appeared in the following websites, literary journals and anthologies: *Ja Magazine (2017), Naane Le Moya (2017), Sol Plaatje European Union Poetry Anthology (2017 & 2018), Kalahari review (2017), Atlanta review (2018), Best 'New' African Poets (2017), Lost lovers anthology (2018).*

Surviving Loss
Busisiwe Mahlangu

Ukusinda:
a) Ukuphepha engozini
b) Ubunzima bento ikalwa

– *Injula nokujiya kwesiZulu, O.L. Shange*

Contents

What is a sin?

I want to tell mama what they've done to me at church
but I fear hell
so I do not speak.

Forgetting home

1.

You are big now;
big can say goodbye with a full mouth
big can carry a suitcase up the stairway
big doesn't run away,
it walks.

2.

You are not leaving anyone behind;
you are leaving an old memory
of a wound's pus
marked on your pillow
next to the map of tears –
the crumbling moments
soaked in vinegar water.
You will learn new ways of healing,
you will learn to pray to God in English
and He will listen.

3.

Once, you could fit your whole body into a pair of hands,
where would you carry yourself now?
Pack your body with you,
cut the unnecessary bits first
be light.

Tear the guilt from your ducts
and clean your blood off your hands.
ubaba passed on,
he was not killed –
especially not by you.

4.

Of all the ghosts you hoard in your throat,
self-doubt screams the loudest
broken bottles on wet grass
are not you
broken bottles on open roads
are not you
broken bottles on the floor
are not the one ubaba broke into your body.

5.

You are a collection of dreams
and faults being rectified.
When the light bulb died,
umama knew your birth would bring a new ray
of beginnings.
You are an answered prayer.
You want to escape.

6.

Start here.
Fold a shirt into a grasshopper.
Fold trousers into a new journey.
Pack a bag for your freedom.

Lost shelves

The pages are missing inside my grandmother   torn
and wet memory washed away   There are stories
she keeps on her fingertips   Tucking them in under
her nails each night

Her name falls off her tongue –   another page
snatched out of her book   Her back is the spine
curling into a rainbow   the only reminder she has
that the freedom promised came   although it forgot us

My grandmother forgot   she is a book without
language   she is history cleaned off the floors
She holds an empty page   her life is   a blank
on a sheet   a pause   a quiet between the wind
Her husband reminds her of their wedding day
playing the moment back with a song
she remembers the bells and the ginger beer
but not his name   not his face   she only knows
his voice   it belongs to a man who once touched her
bones   moved to their breaking

We fill the space with the past   We condense
seventy years inside a four-roomed house

We are holding grandmother's face close to her eyes
We watch her turn from paper to tree   and all that
she lost is just leaves   and this is autumn
Have you seen an empty library breathe?

Moving the air around it to survive   Ever seen
a book that can't be read   A line you cannot colour into
Have you ever seen dementia in a body   Ever lived
a life you cannot point at

Between the shelves in the library

I hold the books that know the place my grandmother sunk
into   every line I read is the language she lost   The
language lost is replaced   with terms and symptoms
that bend better in English   Alzheimer's is writing a new
book with her body without her voice

She is holding the air like that   like one day her body will
disappear like her mind did   She is enveloping her words
in steel   engraving herself somewhere   grandmother
watching pages of her diary float off her body

Grandma, there is still a book that has your name clear on the
cover

I am a book that will never forget you   I will never forget you

What the man stole

he cracked my mother's spine

wrapped it with a ten rand note

took her everywhere

left her behind each time

After School

The boy in my class   carries a knife in his bag
        He says it is only sharp enough to cut apples

When night comes
He stands under a peach tree
                         With his shadow hiding
Looks for apples
             Finds them in a woman's purse
               Sometimes between thighs
                  His blade cuts through the branches

Tomorrow the man who saw him laughs
          The humour is boys who never lose
                 their shadows in the dark –
        And men with no honour in the dark –

Boys who grow up to be scary men. Like him.
I can feel the laughter on every street holding a knife

Is the man laughing about the knife
               or the boy who taught it to cut apples?

If your father was a nightmare

You want to ask your father
why everything sounds dead on his tongue
before you can
he calls your name three times.
He kills you
and pours the remains back into your body.

He says his name twice
he dies   and jumps into a grave.
You are his grave.
At night he is tumbling into your walls.
Your face is a closing door.
Your mouth is on the floor open.
You try to hold onto the floor
but it leaves you like everyone
did.
You stand up so quickly you disappear.

Wash me with fire

I think you must be a body of fire
  to survive being burnt.
Avoid being wood
  or plastic
  or flesh
or water
You must have feet that run on wind.
You must disguise into a flame
  and the fire will miss you.
The month a man shrunk himself to embers,
  our shack burnt to ash.
Ubaba saw how fire can end shame.
He poured paraffin over the wood
  tossed a lit match.
I cannot claim to have mourned.
A house doesn't dance the same way
  a body does inside death.
When we rebuilt we became cautious of sparks.
Placed the paraffin stove outside and used it there.
umama did not trust ubaba to stay away
  from negotiating our exit.
To be a body of fire
  you should not let heat collapse you.
She built our house with bricks and cement.
  ubaba's anger could not gaslight any room.

Escape

Next to her grandma
she is the daughter that swallowed rain and lightning.
and still lived

Next to the wall
she is a corner safe from any flood

Next to herself
she is a puddle on the floor.
almost not there

[1]note

---

1   *There are characters I will not stop writing until I know they will live.*

Solitude

you make
your friends
ghosts

they haunt you
with the silence
you taught them

Process

You are collecting yourself from old things that are fading. Age behind dust. You are looking for yourself in all the roads you built with your feet. Some paths were already there. Some you shaped with your hands. And the thorns remained as a reminder. Some of your footprints are filled with mud. You cannot see them without breaking your back. You are tired. Tired feels like slowly wilting. Tired means rest your bones for now. In your rest, you begin to count all the things you lost to the mud. The spoon you used to eat gravy. Your first kiss. The straps of your bra. Your ninth finger. Someone. Everyone. Yourself. You count loss until you are the ash. You cry. Ash becomes wet. Ash never becomes paste. You fold into a ball and learn to survive alone. You don't go anywhere without checking if you are leaving yourself. You hurt and you don't have any words to say it. Someone stabbed you. Drove you to this place. Your footprints are not on the ground. Your body is under your bed. You are learning sleep again. On the thirtieth day, you are still teaching your eyes how to close. Stay there. Heal. Go outside. Heal. Don't move. Heal. Do what healing calls you to do. Sometimes it won't call you to do anything

Paint your left foot red
and your right, green.
a woman needs emergency signs
to go
running at 5pm.

Boy breaking

This boy is fixing what he broke

                    But what he broke is not a thing

He broke the door

                        I was just behind it

He broke the table

                          I was under it

He broke the cup

                    I was drinking from it
                              I spilled

The roof is leaking

                    I think he broke it too

He is touching everything
With blood on his fingers

                        I think he broke

But he doesn't want to shatter
He is collapsing inside
His kisses are sharp excuses
When he is gone, it's okay

                  When I am gone, it's okay

We are breaking somewhere else
This boy tries to repair everything

                    I want to reward him with love

Even when his lungs are leaking air

                    I say, he is just a crack
                And I know where to find tape
                    I say, I've never seen anyone
              fall apart like a flower opening
     I say, his love for me begins at the end of every outbreak

This boy is fixing what he broke
but what he broke is not a thing

-

---

2   *Fixing a boy makes me forget I am broken.*

Fixing a daughter

                                   With the same sharp hand
                              she presses the creases on his pants,
                              she scrubs the darkness off my back.

The smell of Dettol
the sound of gospel
fill the room with renewal
                    She watches the shadow that grew under my arms
Stretching backwards
Clinging to my neck
                         Maybe this daughter doesn't want to be saved
                              that is why she let the dirt stay on her skin

A sack of oranges
opening the pores of a wound
leaving red skin burning
                                   This cleansing is slow drowning
The gospel bidding goodbye

                                        she peels layers off
                                   Until I am old sex again

I beg

Coat my body with Vaseline or oil
moisturise the scabs
Coat the soles of my feet with floor polish
Let me smell of candles and paraffin

Fold me back to a kiss before the water broke

My begging is swallowed
by the scratching
and nails digging into me

When it all stops
I am wearing new Christmas clothes
he is wearing freshly ironed pants

She couldn't scrub his hands off me

[3]Birthmarks

---

3   *My mother's mother has done this suffering for my mother*
           My mother has done this suffering for me
               This is how I inherit a scar

Rusty Knife

She taught me how to look well   Or how to be well   I don't
remember which one it was
But I learnt that happiness is found in practice

My aunt peels an onion   with her hands   Tomorrow she smells
the loss in them   Whispers, 'the war is not over'   Holds the knife
like a sword   and starts cooking   The knife is rusty and old   We
never think of replacing it   or ourselves   We are rusty and old
a thousand years around our eyes   learning joy in a pot

The vegetables desired saving too   and the meat   that is forced
to feed all of us   is tired of being the sacrifice   I can see my
aunt   almost chopping off her fingers   for food that is thrown
onto the floor   I almost ask, 'what does this man eat   When
he is playing Frisbee with the plates?'

But uncle believes in magic   In food growing from the kitchen
cupboards   and peace that replies to his outrage   When you look
into his eyes   you cannot see death coming   you can see death
going   Following the swing plates take before breaking   And
behind, my aunt with a half-smile

Halfway well   Picking up the pieces   with a shield built of fabled
bliss   Ready to burst

loss

there are few spaces where i can breakdown.

and heal.

i am afraid

they are   collapsing

too.

Alone

I

If the sky falls
and crushes the ladybug in my hand
I will mourn first its life
then mourn my solitude.

Every time it thunders,
I lose something I blew my secrets into.
The storm takes everything
leaves me standing
watching an end.

The last time I kissed a boy I cried,
he was filled with air
I could feel him float out of my arms.

II

I am more ashamed of my loneliness
than I am of my sadness.

The women without men are called witches
or accused of killing their men
if they are widows.

When a boy floats, I hold his jacket
He was alive before he left.
He did not run away, he flew.

This is evidence.

III

My sadness can fill half a lung
and I will not complain about breathing

I've learnt to wait slowly for death
with someone holding my hand.

But now, there is no hand laying on my mine.
I am afraid I will have to sing the hymn myself
for heaven to receive me.

IV

Someone said,
Loneliness is how a spirit slowly leaves a body.
It bids goodbye by clutching onto flesh.

I have enough time to love another boy
and another
all at once
But boys make me feel temporary and unloved.

I wonder,
How they treat their loneliness
With this constant shifting.

My body spells happy different

i.

How many mouths can you trust with your name?/
How many hands can you trust with your body?

ii.

I remember you shrunk./ Crumbling when words became
stones./
They hit your knock-knees and stopped the kissing./
You learnt to walk while falling apart.

iii.

You make a wish on your face./ You pop a zit./ You scar
yourself
to measure the time healing takes./ After years of scratching
pimples,
you know./ Calling your skin ugly/ will not make it go away.

iv.

The advert on the television/ said, "give us your scars, we will
hide them"./
You tucked your cellulite into your jeans/
wrapped a scarf around your chest./ You went to the shop/
and bought *Bio-Oil* under disguise.

v.

There is always someone suggesting a way to fix yourself./
There is a way to make tummy-rolls roll off you./
There is a way to burn the bulge under your arm./
There is a way to cut your hips./
There is a bra that can hold your breasts to your chin./
There is a way to exit your body.

vi.

You can start running/ from all the mouths that want to swallow
your body like a fault./ You can start running from yourself/
when you are holding a spade to collapse the fault./
Remember that you own one body./
This is not a suggestion.

vii.

How many parts of you do you let your mouth speak?/
How many parts of you do you let your hands hold?

Worship

My body holds a song, stands still while the waves rise and fall
in places locked away.

The music is a call for freedom.

An anthem inside throats with half prayers.

In my body, there are cities that have stopped waiting for a hymn

and started burning their temples,

made holy a body of ashes,

made fire a circle of faith.

Now bricks float in the air like dust. I play the song with my
fingers:

the labia a plain instrument

the clitoris a string

I know how to move dead cities.

There is magic in my body that loneliness cannot empty out.

Do not touch me like you are digging a girl out of a grave

I have saved myself through orgasms

over the gospel and the preaching.

Pleasure is holy. Do not waste it on your ego.

I deserve a God who will not call this worship a sin.

Who will not call my hands inside my jar stealing.

I am not waiting for a husband. I am waiting for a chord

that will strike my spine to dance.

I am naked when I read the Bible,
this is how I pray and sing worship.
This is how I return to my body.
There are abandoned places in me
that only I can rescue

God!
I will call your name
when I come

Magic Wonder

My mother is a woman

who gossips about herself,

she laughs

and her bones fall back into place.

She pulls out a girl stuck in a man's broken rib.

Teaches the girl how to swim in her blood

after they killed her.

She knows that she is the girl.

Places her gums on the table

before they pull out her teeth.

The women I grew out of

laugh to feel they are still here.

They open their mouths

tell their stories

and vomit tales they were forced to believe.

Your wound is growing into a person
you can touch your pain
and tell it to let you go.

Scraps

I know about the taking that having nothing does
and poverty that drowns a name
and replaces it with begging

and hands that are strong enough to overturn the world
but they are too full of grease from fixing falling things

I was born in a place where people mourn lost jobs like sons who die
follow them in the mud and beg the grave to swallow them whole

The weight of breathing in a body is the end of life
The bend of a spine rolling over the floor
Leaving a dirt that water cannot wash away

Finding a job is finding a slaughterhouse.

Loss has hands and legs and a pulse
Loss is the number of heads next to a burning tire
Loss has a bullet in its chest

Sometimes the country forgets to apologise
Sometimes we apologise for the protest and the smoke
We have to apologise for speaking.

This is the place you never leave

Reincarnation

The wrinkled city will not die without reviving its people,
Marabastad, Pretoria greasy from holding onto life.

The old pile of clothes sits after crawling out of a grave,
the street will not let penniless hangers go cold.

We come here in rags
to thrift a jacket, a skirt or jeans,
something someone has danced in for years
before owning something better.
You are taught to move quickly,

To hold the coins in your hand tightly
To buy any jersey that fits you even if you don't like the colour.
Every time we return from shifting our bodies past the crowds
I am left with damp faces of vendors in my eyes.
A deep wanting to feel something new on my skin.

The sun still burns my pockets dry.
And I will always remember that someone once loved these rags.

Soldiers come home from war

with their last breath jumping from finger to finger
counting whose son died in the front

and was left behind like litter. Their palms exuding expectations
ready to celebrate a second-hand freedom

but their limbs are cut out by chains. Gunshots convincing minds
to believe in a tangible reality,

they vowed before the nose of a breathless pistol
that they will live to see roses blooming out of concrete.

They crawl with their legs falling behind,
throw their eyes to the distance of burnt houses

they call home. No one told them that soldiers
are useless? Only meant to breathe on the battlefield?

After war, the fighting never stops. They are found hanging
from a branch of a tree behind their burnt homes.

soldiers come home from war.
soldiers come home to war.

Safe house

the old chair is pushed against the door/ the windows are closed/
the gate is locked/ the fence has barbed wire to hook the flesh/
a good night's sleep is bought with *"caution"*:/ pull all the keys
out of the doors/
do not switch off the lights/ turn over the welcome mats/ tell the
dog to start barking

since they can steal from a body too/ I sat in the old chair behind
the door,/
I built windows with bricks/ I wrapped a chain and lock around
the gate,/
I have a scar on my leg from the fence/ every breath is taken with
caution:/
swallow the keys after locking/ pretend to be awake/ burn all the
welcome mats/ teach the dog how to bite

we spent our lives waiting for thieves to come/ but they live in our
house

Violation

My anger is a log in a fire
Did not start the flame but burned
Soon, there will be no one to blame when I turn to ash

The inferno in my chest is a prison
a person who's hurt before cannot do it again
I have them drink the fuel they poured on my feet

This anger did not start the flame
but that explosion is all of it. All of me

My anger burnt my tears
My anger moulded my chest a shield
My anger taught my breath to be gasoline
No one fought for me, my anger did
Fought for the women in my blood
The children
never touch the fire but they feel the warmth

This is protection
This is a volcano erupting to save us

House

When the police come to arrest him
tell them to put handcuffs on the door,
this house is a culprit
watching us bleed without moving.
The first time he turned beast,
the walls collapsed our screams into a song
the neighbours danced to the sharp melody.
This house
will watch us get killed and say nothing.

The walls wear our blood like paint
our DNA washes off into colour,
it is a battle
with only one boxing champion.
Constantly we break through kitchen tiles
we slowly rise to our knees,
we are learning prayer
with the ceiling slapping our words back onto our tongues

As if to say,

what we are asking for

is a different kind of heaven. One that we will never reach,

where men don't molest women,

where houses are not ghosts,

where fathers love their daughters,

where fathers love.

This house will watch us get killed,

the floor will swallow our skeletons.

This house is a graveyard

dry bones pull us back when we walk

our suitcases decay before we can pack our bags to leave.

There is a memorial service in each room

old obituaries hanging like curtains

windows open to wave life goodbye.

Those who came before us never touched victory.

Those who came before us were us.

We have touched death every evening.
We have bled out eulogies and goodbyes
but today the police are coming.

And if we are dead when they get here

tell them

to put handcuffs on the door.

This house is a culprit

watching us die.

Investigations

Did your father die or did he leave?

Did your father call you by name or not call at all?

Did your father become the wind?

Vanity

A rose died without releasing its fragrance, or you were too late to smell its perfume.

Can you sit down and apologize? Place your feet on the ground and start digging graves, what else can you do with all the dead things you see?

Will you cry at the funeral? It is only a rose, the tenth one you tried to save in a week. You cried at every funeral you went to. Sometimes you did not leave your bedroom to attend to the dead.

Will you put up a tombstone? Find a big rock in the garden to remind you, the pink rose is laying here. Or a rose that lost all its petals is there – waiting for a name.

Whose name will you write? Yours? You are mending the soil. You are managing drought. You don't know which name now. You can play scrabble with yours later.

Last question,
all these roses you want to hide from your eyes,
do you know you can't stop burying your father?

Fathers who are water

The candle burns, brushes away darkness, everything is connected to light.

A family sits around the table and their presence seals the holes of a shack with a moonbeam. Light settles on their plates and they enjoy a meal.

I know a girl who will never understand what that means.

She is what the flames left behind.
Fire comes to die on her cold tongue.
In her heart, everything is swallowed by darkness.
Her father's absence is smoke and her mother is rubbing ash on her chest – fixing a broken heart.
Her father was water but the wind drank him up.

his absence is ice.

She pulls men into her body to feel the cold,
she wants their heat to stay inside her
but all the men she has touched are corpses, always leaving a trail of snow
on her pillow.

his life becomes a pause in your lungs.

We are daughters who never stop searching
who always have their eyes up in the skyline,
drawing possible faces of fathers
we've never met.
We are grounded chimneys and flying smoke,
we are what the flames left behind.
Fire comes to die on our cold tongues,
the smoke comes out frozen saying
I had a father who was water but the wind drank him up.
My father is the air but I cannot go through him.

His absence is steam.

In a culture where men do not stay with their families,
men wander off to evaporate.
We become children who are chasing the flood
writing love letters to the ocean for we don't know where our fathers live,
only that when they left, the candle stopped burning.

Sometimes, I want to ask mom what *dad* looked like
but I can imagine her carving him out of stillness.
His eyes outlined by the dark,
he has no face, his whole body is water
and next time I see him
he will be on my mother's face
walking out on her again.
I never cry along, tears remind me of men who are gone.

whose absence is ice and have names built out of steam.
Whenever it rains my father returns,
still without a face but a body of liquid.
He waters our garden and soaks into the ground.

he is never coming back.

I don't know if he is out there.
I don't know if he is alive.
but I am.

Look at yourself
you have not died yet
you are an unending revolution
you are surviving loss

Unbecoming

My body is small and pain lives there. Ever since the storm,
pain flooded out of its place and looked for home.
This escape is not intentional.
It is an interruption for both of us. Pain is a glitch in my blood
with its quest.
I am a glitch with my small body. To evict pain is to evacuate too.
We fall into a routine of
temporary survival; pins and needles under my skin, the roof
leaks, I seal it with flesh.
When all flesh is wound, I use gum. My body gets smaller.
Pain grows.
My body coils into itself and becomes a tenant.
Pain is small but my body lives there.

Needles

I hope they sew the heavy stench of placenta away
before they stitch my lips into a silent prayer.

Each breath taken feels like a failed attempt.
All the thread I owned left with a man with shovel hands.

On the hospital bed I want to die.
to forget.
But the needles sing a song I cannot hear past my waist.
The doctor says I have a son.

I want to tell her to kill him before he grows shovel hands

but his eyes blink in apology.
He fights not to look like a fault.
I fight not to look.

My insides were opened twice
that night   and today
by people who never asked me if I wanted a son.

⁴Rescue

4   *when the sun sets again*
      blow the whistle
      and signal for help

Questions

What are you losing?
What still remains?

Less

I open my eyes and see half   of everything I look at:

the glass on the table is filled to the middle,   while the other
half is broken.   the table is
smaller than before   and our house is left with one room.

my father walks into the room   with some of his mistakes.   he
shrank his way to forgiveness
with his left side stuck in the past.   today he is the right man my
mother loved.

we spend our days happy.   half ourselves.   selflessly on the
clock.   we stop digging each other's graves.
we don't hurt enough to start   preparing for death.

I can teach you how to feel pain less:

flail your eyelid   use half your pupil   close your
other eye
this is the best way   to run away   from home without
leaving.

River

Near the end of a song,
I am not ready to stop this dance with you

> Tell me
> you will sing with your mouth
> Tell me
> you will summon time to wait for us
> Tell me
> good things that don't end don't rot

Pour the song out of your body like a river

This is yours

This is how you return to yourself
This is the sound
This is the blast
Take the silence no one hears
This is how you return to yourself
This is your reflection on the glass
These are parts that broke but are still here
This is the collapse and the rebuilding
This is a tasteless resurrection
This is how you make home with your body
This is how you return to yourself
This is how you fit into happiness
This is the gap for your escape
This is you being carried by wind
This is how you hold your lungs to the air
This is how you breathe through every wound
This is how you hold yourself

This is you, here
This is you, breathing
This is you, healing

This is how your soul tells you, you are doing well.

Cuddling

Are we helping each other escape?
What do you mean when you hold me?
Did you see me become the floor?
Is that the reason you fell over?
You want crumble into something calm?
I can open
You can disappear
inside
a well
or an empty ocean.
I am not your wound.
I am void.

new affirmations for the past

and one day the wind blows our way again,
we do not ask it where it comes from and what it carries
we let it move the soil and bend the trees
we watch it become stronger

here is a moment:
maybe we can tell the wind to go back
maybe we prepare better for the current
maybe i pull the clothes off the washing line on time
and i close all the windows
before the wind pulls the door from its hinges

and all the children live
and mama has open arms to embrace us all

Busy

When you burn the food for supper   you are saying   you are
tired

     (exhausted, finished, borrowed)

You are saying your body   is an accident   with broken bones
and tired wrists

    (cracking inside doings, ignoring collapse,
       postponing emergency)

Your mother shouts at you   because you are surrendering   to
the voices stringing you
 out of your skin

     (It is rescue, with her body, her voice)

This kitchen becomes you   half washed cups in the cabinet
pots with their burning
waiting for another sacrifice

(inadequate but functional, inadequate and functional, inade-
quate, a functional mistake)

The cracking sounds like a pelvis. It is new life you yearn for
that must heal you

   (planning for breath, raising a daughter from misery,
     watch her find happy)

If you stretch your body   you will not feed it ash   anymore, feed
it air and your lover's word

  (building a body,   a lover will stay,   but not for you)

Every time someone exits you   they leave the door open
for your escape and for the smoke
to settle

  (lungs on fire,   supper on fire,   this burning is undesirable)

Your home is a house   with tools for dying   you practice
death on the stove
you practice death when you laugh

    (a routine,   a habit,   a cover up)

When you go they will remember you like this   burnt food and
shattering plates
they will not mention your bones collapsing   they did not hear
that

    (be a memory,   happy,   forgetful mess)

They were just eating your bowl of fire   no one noticed you
went cold   you always coated
your goodbyes   with soft love

    (rest,   sleep,   put your tools down)

Today I am a victim

Tomorrow I am a survivor

Some days I am both

It doesn't undo the crime

Come with air

Loss is inevitable. Nothing can be done.

I will not mourn a thing. I will not disappear.

When my bed is a mouth with a thousand teeth,
I am a loss, and a thing chewed to its end.
My breath clings onto grief.

Wake up

                  "The water is boiling; won't you make some tea?"
My baby sister will ask
with lightning striking from her chest
carving anger out of a throat filled with trumpets, screaming
because the truth will always be a lie
If not a lie
then it will always be a knife cutting through her heart

Outside, the water has been eating flames for more than an hour
now
Our fire is a phantom star about to close its eyes
but we have to keep the fire burning
The wise men might miss the stars
but the flames will let them know that we have been waiting on
God for years
We have been waiting on God!

My sister is seven, I am eleven
our house has been standing on our young shoulders for years
The August wind bumped the side of our home
Our shaking shack is now handicapped on frozen wheels
not moving
we cannot afford to move
We wait and hope that those who can, will find us here
I hope you find us, here

If you do, please do not ask to us to dance for you
We lost our legs to the cold
Poverty ate away our feet
so we don't follow the footsteps of our parents
                   You want to know why our food is dirty?

We plant our fingers on wet soil
to grow extra hands, to put food on the table
We cannot offer you a glass of water
but you can take our sad faces for your thirst
We don't chew bones under this roof
there are pieces of our broken selves lying everywhere
You might choke on our blood
or stumble on a ribcage
but don't tell them that we are dodging death every evening
The candle watches us with caution
The dead bodies that have burned down with the squatter camp
will beg us to wake

> "Wake up, why
> won't you wake
> up?"

We are scared of drowning!
There is a flood in the kitchen, devouring the flames

I did not come to this stage by choice
I was swept by the tide while sleeping
I don't want to wake up because I will have to watch myself die if
do

Tell my sister:

I cannot change water into tea

Tell her:

You gave me snaps and applause
When all I was asking was a loaf of bread
And all   I am asking is a loaf of bread
A mother in your pockets
A father under your jacket
Salt in your hands

What about that
loaf of bread?

I don't need it anymore
My body has built a home out of hunger
Is standing by the side of the robot
saying   please

Because what are stories worth?

Acknowledgements

Sis' vangile gantsho, thank you for pulling this book out of me, I did not know I had it inside me. Thank you for helping me craft these stories, you put glitter on my face, always. Sarah Godsell, you gave me fairy dust long before you gave me fairy dust. I met you as my poetry teacher, you've grown to be more in my life, thank you for giving me air and for holding me. You are magic, you teach me gentleness and softness in a world that has spikes everywhere. Tanya Pretorius, you see me and you draw me all up. Thank you for the best fitting cover for *Surviving Loss* and for covering my head with hair, I will always remember this. **impepho press**; Sis'vangi, Sarah and Tanya, I love you, thank you for making space for my voice and for allowing me the privilege of growing with you. May **impepho press** be the dream that has been shown to you and more. Makubongwe. Camagu!

Mama, ngiyabonga. Izifiso zami namaphupho ami ayafezeka ngoba uyakholelwa kuwo futhi uyangisekela. Lencwadi iyincwadi ephathekayo namuhla ngenxa yakho mama wami. Uyisibusiso, ngiyathandaza ukuthi yonke imithandazo yakho iphendulwe. You taught me how to read and write, you've given me this gift. Thulani, your resilience and bravery are inspiring, you make me believe in the life of dreams. Jabulile, my big sister, I still cry in public. You've taught me that strength has many colours. May your heart be lighter, you have all the time you need. Nosimo, watching you growing up has been evidence that God exists. I want to protect you all the time but I know that God and our father watches over you. You never ask for permission to be. Growing up with you all is my favourite childhood story, I love you all.

Bab'mncane, for the number of times you've rescued me, I am here. I love you.

To my teacher, Mr Kekana, you are a gift to Mamelodi and to Gatang Secondary School, thank you for your time and your teachings and for bringing us to the world of literature. You introduced me to poetry and you've helped me greatly with the penning of this book. Mrs Malatji Mareka and Mrs Mphuthi, thank you for your love and support.

To Phillippa Yaa de Villiers, think you for hearing me and for seeing me.

Lwazilubanzi Project: Ofentse Dibakwane, Thapelo Nyaps and Tc, thank you for not thinking I am crazy when I pitched that we start an NPO and run Creative Writing workshops in schools. Your work, commitment and support in this dream has kept me going.

Gontse Tshabalala, the world will hear you and your gift. I believe this.

Nomasonto, I've watched you break free from fear many times, there are no limits for you.

Refilwe, you write beautifully, you sing amazingly, you are a blessing.

Mmorongwa, keep on painting rainbows everywhere you want, don't stop imagining.

To my friends, thank you for your love and the ways you inspire me: Nthabeleng Lesoli, Xolile Mabuza, Siphiwe Cilo, Rethabile Zilila, Mjele Msimang, Anga Mamfanya, Manola Gayatri and Harold Muchengeta. I love you all.

I would like to thank movements/companies/poetry houses that have been/are part of my journey: Hear My Voice, Speak Out Loud, Mzansi Poetry Academy, National Library of South Africa, Voice of Kasi Katz, Current State of Poetry, Lingua Franca, Grounding Sessions, Words in My Mouth and many stages that have housed me and grew me.

I am grateful for all that inspires me. Thank you for being here.

TITLES

feeling & ugly by danai mupotsa

Liquid Bones by Sarah Godsell

red cotton by vangile gantsho

Printed in the United States
By Bookmasters